RECITATIONS

BY

RUSTICUS

PRINTED FOR THE AUTHOR,
BY THEW & SON, HIGH STREET, KING'S LYNN.
MDCCCXCVIII.

TO

HELEN

I INSCRIBE

THIS LITTLE VOLUME

WITH MY LOVE.

INDEX

FAITHFUL BEN

A friend of mine had a bulldog, Ben,
Who was famous among the dogs of men;
One shake was enough for a couple of cats,
One nip would have killed a pailful of rats;
He'd a weakness, too, for rounded calves
And he didn't attempt to do things by halves,
Except that his teeth were apt to divide
The tendons to which they were firmly applied.
Yes, Ben was an awkward fellow to tackle—
There isn't a hen or a goose that dare cackle
Within a mile of his frown or his smile,
Nor is there a dog but his tail at once drops
At sight of our Ben, his teeth and his chops,
And between his hind legs submissively stops.

Yet Ben, be it said, of his own master stood
In such awe as a well-bred doggy should;
A word sufficed to bring him to heel,
And he'd "kennel up" sharp at every meal,
Content with a sniff at some succulent viand
Which he well understood might be his by-&-bye, and,
If he didn't lie quiet, a different diet,
Composed of the stick, or maybe a kick,
Would be all that he'd get, however sharp-set,
For greediness oftentimes ends in regret.

'Twas a breezy day at the close of May,
When the wind was a trifle inclined to be "stingy,"
In homely phrase, and the ocean was dingy,
For the sand and the sea by a passing gale
Had been frothily mixed as though threshed by a flail,
All which to my friend didn't matter a button,
Nor yet to our Ben, who—the wicked old glutton!—
Had just made a meal of a farmyard duck,
Without having waited for Sarah to pluck
The feathers and down that from tail to crown
Close-matted the bird.—So out the two trudged—

Without his master Ben wouldn't have budged—
And wended their way to the sad seashore
As much for a blow as anything more ;
But when they arrived my friend thought this—
" By Jingo ! it won't be so very amiss
If I hurriedly strip for one little dip ;
We're out of sight of those bathing machines,
Which are only fit for girls in their teens,
And I shall be dressed—or sufficiently so—
Before any people are likely to know
That for once I've transgressed the bye-regulations
Which are often the curse of our civilised nations."

So his clothes he doffed and speedily had 'em
Rolled up in a heap and stood as was Adam
Before that fall which did for us all,
And, after he'd given his dog an injunction
To mind his clothes, having little compunction
In breaking those bye-laws, he plunged in the ocean
And made as much rout and stir and commotion
As if he were some old porpoise or shark
Careering around for a bit of lark

And just as they were—naked—stark !

The water was cold and he didn't stay long
Though an expert swimmer, stout-hearted and strong ;
But what was his great surprise and wonder
To hear his dog, Ben, make a noise like thunder
When he turned for his clothes—" Don't you know me,
    Ben ? "
He said with a laugh, which died away when
Ben slowly exhibited grinders four
With a strong extending under-jaw
That suggested a rat trap screwed to a vice
In a way that was certainly far from nice.

My friend could scarcely believe his eyes
And was shaking all over with cold and surprise ;
That his faithful Ben should decline to know him
And a bristling row of canines show him
Was absurd, of course, and exceedingly droll,
Though not to him just then—on the whole—
But there it was, and there he stood
Trying all the seductive devices he could

To find his way out of that thorny wood;
But coax and wheedle, whistle and call,
Storm and threaten and rage and bawl,
His Ben didn't care one snap for it all;
His response was a growl and a threatening glare,
As much as to say, " Come on if you dare ! "

'Twas an awkward predicament, none can deny;
In Adam's dress, one is fain to confess,
It was really out of the question to fly;
And there wasn't a decent-sized stone within reach
The faithful Ben his duty to teach;·
The bravest man might very well quail
In attacking a dog with a kink in his tail,
A sign you must know of high-class breeding,
But my friend at that moment was scarcely heeding
The points of his dog—he only regretted
He'd ever set eyes on him, much more petted
So stupid a brute—Bah !—To make such a choice
Of a dog that knew not his own master's voice,
And what is still stranger—not even his scent,

Which my friend must have carried wherever he
    went !—

'Tis a way that dogs have, though I don't know their
    plan,

For the clothes go too often to make up the man.

Now the dog was lying provokingly cool,

His head on his paws, as still as a pool

On a soft summer's day ; so my friend inclined

To try and approach his clothes from behind.

He made a circuit and stealthily crept,

As his too faithful hound apparently slept,

By inches nearer—could he only get hold

Of his dear old breeches—he was shaking with cold—

When just as he seemed in reach of his store

Ben darted round with an ominous roar

And rushed straight away for the calves of his legs,

Which caused my friend to spin round on his pegs

And fly with all the speed he could carry—

For he hadn't the means this attack to parry—

And the dog meant business—that was quite clear—

So away he went like a nimble deer

With Ben at his heels intent on his calves,
For he wasn't a dog to do things by halves.

My friend, as it chanced, was a bit of a sprinter
And had won an occasional prize in the winter;
So he managed to keep just ahead of the hound
As they ran at full speed o'er the soft sandy ground;
But alas! every stride brought him nearer to those
Confounded machines, where the inmates in hose,
All modest and proper, were in and out popping,
But my friend couldn't think for a moment of stopping.
For Ben towards his calves was still inclined
And was not more than one or two fathoms behind,
While, to make things worse, two stalwart policemen,
Apprehenders of those of our kind who would fleece
    men,
Appeared from afar and straightway came
To see for themselves my friend's little game;
And so, poor man, like the French at Sedan,
From front and from rear he was hardly attacked
And at his wits' end to know how to act.

" Of two or three evils choose the lesser ; "

'Tis a very wise maxim ; who'll be the assessor

To say on the spur of the moment of three

Which the least of these evils is going to be ?

My friend, having run a considerable distance,

Had fixed on the line of the least resistance ;

That wasn't the bobbies—you may wager on that—

They'd have knocked him into a full general's hat ;

Nor was it the hound, still intent on his calves

Who never attempted to do things by halves ;

No ! my friend, driven now to the point of despair,

Espied a machine, that was one of a pair,

With the door wide open, and without taking thought

What might result should he chance to be caught,

He dashed within and slammed the door,

Then dropped down exhausted upon the floor.

I am almost afraid to depict the scene

Enacted around that bathing machine.

Three elderly ladies were dressing inside,

Who, rather than meet a strange man, would have
    died ;

And who, when they this apparition espied
Dashing up the stairs, all unawares,
Rushed out at the back in costumes unique
Of which it scarcely becomes me to speak,
To whom Ben at once transferred his affection,
For to ladies' legs he'd no sort of objection.
Then try to imagine it, if you can,
The shrieks and the cries, as the ladies ran
As fast as they could, especially when
They heard behind them the snorting of Ben,
And the shouts of the bobbies and yells of the crowd,
Who unkindly gave vent to their feelings aloud
Till my poor friend wished himself into his shroud.

But all things that have a limit must cease ;
The bobbies at length restored them to peace ;
With the aid of their truncheons they smartly
    succeeded
In staying our Ben, whose career they impeded
With a blow on the head which laid him half dead ;
Then they turned to my friend who had meanwhile
    shut,

For modesty's sake, the back door of the hut,
And shouted out " What is the meaning of this, sir ?
You're aware you've behaved extremely amiss, sir ? "
To whom my friend said in response to their screeches,
" Good fellows, for mercy's sake fetch me my breeches,
My boots and my shirt, that lie within reach
A few hundred paces away on the beach ! "

To prolong the agony's not artistic,
And, my friend being not of a turn pugilistic,
I will simply state that having obtained
The breeches, of which he chiefly complained,
That is, of their loss, he soon came out
Of the hut which had been the scene of the rout,
And surrendered himself to the brave defenders
Of laws that so urgently need good emenders ;
And when he had offered his explanation
With many apologies for the vexation
He'd caused to those elderly ladies, he
Was allowed by the bobbies to go scot free,
Having given his name, should the local authority
Apply for a summons ; but though the minority

Of councillors favoured that course the majority
Declined to punish my friend again
For what was clearly the fault of his Ben;
The moral of which is—remember your hose
Has the strongest attraction for a dog's nose,
Who's inclined to resent a condition of nudity
As being 'mongst civilised people a crudity;
And, since there are those who think that our dress
Is the one thing needful for man to possess,
Mrs. Grundy's rules 'tis unwise to transgress.

THE UNMENTIONABLES

The story of the hapless wight
  Who went to bathe and had his clothes
Filched by some devilish imp or sprite
  Is catalogued among the woes
  That belong of right to mankind's hose.

The story, too, of the citizen
Who took as a guard his bull-dog, Ben,
Which, seeing his panting master emerge
From out the dripping salt and surge,
Declined to know him in the dress
That Nature had provided—less
The poor man scarcely could possess—
And barked and bit and drove him off
Amid the laughing neighbours' scoff—
I think the fun has already been spun

And needs not afresh to be recorded,
Although the tale is rightly belauded
For all the amusement it's afforded.

My story runs in a similar groove
Which I trust my hearers will kindly approve,
And as I am bound to deal in "conventionables"—
   That is, in the vulgar, the strictest propriety—
I have labelled my story above, "The Unmentionables"-
   A word that is used in politest society—
To describe what befell a very dear friend,
Which nearly, you'll see, occasioned his end.

My friend, you must know, had a dog called "Dash,"
   A name derived from his exclamations,
For Dash was determined to made a big splash
   In the world of dogs by his perigrinations;
'Tis right you should know what a mischievous brute
This little dog was—not a slipper or boot,
Not a carpet or rug, not a pillow or sheet,
But was torn or soiled by the little brute's feet
In a way with which no dog could compete.

To get to my story—one day his master,

Not dreaming of aught in the way of disaster,

Went out for a bathe, and Dash went too,

In which there was nothing strange, striking or new ;

But, when my friend had swum well out,

My other friend, Dash, ran sniffing about,

As the spirit of mischief began to infuse him,

For something or other wherewith to amuse him.

He rejected the hat, the coat and the vest

And, thrusting aside the whole of the rest,

He went for the *breeches*—'twas a strange fit of vice—

And—the little varmint !—in less than a trice,

Not caring a rap if the action were nice,

The most mischievous thing he was able to hit upon

And exercise his audacious young wit upon,

He ripped off the legs clean away from the *sit-upon*,

And as skillfully tore the seat to ribbons

As our dear old Church was dissected by Gibbons.

His master returned and began to resume

His apparel without any fussing or fume ;

He put on his vest, he buttoned his shirt,

He pulled on his socks—he felt hungry, voracious,
He noticed that Dash was unusually pert,
  Then he looked for his—"Where on earth?—

                My goodness gracious!

Where on earth are my—? Dash! Have you played
  me a trick?

My dog, 'tis a case—'tis a case of the stick!"
Then he turned and he saw—what made him turn sick—
He saw beyond reach scattered over the beach
A hundred and one tweed-suitable specks—
He knew them, alas! by the size of the checks—
That once had been—what a sight to be seen!—
The seat of his breeches—what was to be done?
Of all the bad businesses—this was the one!

As cats are useless unless they are mousers,
What is the good of a man without *trousers*?
The first thing—my friend of his dog took toll
And added his name to the dogs' death roll,
Which done, he experienced life's bitter dregs
As the wind whistled round the calves of his legs;
For the town was a mile and a half from the shore,

Not a cottage between where one might implore
The loan of some *Bags*—or even a legging—
Not a thing of the sort was going a-begging;
And the road to the town was crowded by all
The élite of the place, like the old-fashioned Mall;
What was to be done? He couldn't stay there
With the wind in the east and his legs all bare;
'Twas a case! he must make up his mind to leg it
As swiftly as ever his poor pins could peg it;
He would fly like a racer, and as for the fun
That others might get—well, all said and done,
They needn't find out—he'd cover his face,
And thus he hoped to avoid the disgrace
And after-effects of his trouserless race.

So he cautiously covered the first half-mile
By taking upon him the savage's wile
And dodging behind each available tree
That lined the path from the road to the sea;
And as soon as he strode full into the road,
He pulled up his coat-tails right over his face
And set off to run at his very best pace.

'Tis hard to describe the exact effect
On each passer-by—but I shrewdly suspect—
Indeed, I am sure—that the most demure
For their want of humour here found a cure,
And held their sides amidst the chaffing
For fear they should split themselves open with
    laughing;
For the wind blew just as gusty along
The hard high road among the throng
As it did on the shore, and to see his shirt tail
Flying out as if it were made for a sail,
Or were hanging to dry on the top of a rail,
Was a sight before which description must pale;
And though one old gentleman made a grimace,
All the dogs and mischievous lads in the place
Set off at a galop to follow the chase;
And the cries and the shouts and barking and noise,
The yelps of the dogs, the yells of the boys,
The shrieks of the girls, the howls of the men,
Quite beggar description and baffle the pen;
But in spite of the clamour, the barks and the brawl,
My friend kept his place at the head of them all,

And eventually reached his destination
Without any mishap or degradation,
Save one mischance at the end of his dance,
For the staid old servant who opened the door
Fell flat on her face and swooned on the floor—
For she'd never—lawks !—seen master's legs before !
But I'm glad to say that none could aver
Whose legs they were that made such a stir,
Though none will forget, you may hazard a crown,
That trouserless race from the shore to the town.

NUGGINS' GHOST

Nuggins had gone to bed quite sober—
   At least he always averred that he did—
In a chilly night in late October;
   And safe beneath the bed clothes hid
He was hugging himself as close and as snug
As the snuggest old bug in the snuggest old rug.

The clock struck twelve, when on the last stroke
   He was startled by feeling a clammy hand
Laid upon him—indeed it was far from a joke,
   As he felt himself gripped in an iron band,
And standing above him he saw a slim ghost
As nearly as tall as a tall bed-post.

To say that he felt in an abject fright
   And shivered and shook from head to heel
Is the state we all in the dead of night
   Might be more or less expected to feel,

But Nuggins lay there in absolute terror,
And that, with a ghost, is surely an error.

He looked at the ghost, and the ghost looked at him
   From the hollow niches that stood for his eyes,
And the smile he gave him was terribly grim—
   That a ghost should smile at all's a surprise,
Yet Nuggins averred of the ghost that he grinned,
And his statement I cannot refute or rescind.

" Get up!—Come with me!—Midnight's past!"
   The ghost gibbered forth with gesture emphatic;
" I'd rather not," answered poor Nuggins aghast,
   "Its warmer up here tucked in bed in this attic!"
" Don't argue the point!" was all the ghost said,
As he rattled his bones round Nuggins' head.

Nuggins would have refused the command had he dared,
   For his teeth could be heard closely chatt'ring a mile off,
'Twas enough, as he afterwards mildly declared,
   To leave a poor fellow with more than one tile off ;
But he followed the ghost down the stairs and the passage
As limp as a man after hot baths and massage.

The passage was draughty and Nuggins' legs
   Were as bare as the bones of that terrible ghost;
'Tis hard to wander on uncovered pegs
   In the dead of night—'twould be better to roast
On the hottest oven that furnace could kindle,
If your legs are as thin as an old lady's spindle.

But off went the ghost and after him trotted
   Joe Nuggins as fast as his poor feet could toe it;
The neighbours must surely have thought him besotted
   When they saw him in night dress so agilely go it,
For the ghost was invisible save to our friend
Who couldn't imagine where this was to end.

They crossed over fields and hedges and ditches,
   The trees looked like skeletons in the dim light,
The air seemed alive with hobgoblins and witches
   And all the queer folk that inhabit the night,
Till at length when beyond his ken they had travelled
Before a deep pond Nuggins found himself gravelled.

The ghost his arm stretched and with a long finger
   He pointed to something that floated upon

The surface—'twas not a nice place to linger
  Or stand about with your night-shirt on ;
But what was there floating upon the pool
Wasn't patent at all, e'en to ghost or to ghoul.

" You notice that body ? " hoarsely whispered the ghost,
  " That carcase is mine "—he continued with awe ;
" I am only a spirit ! " " I know that to my cost,"
  Murmured Nuggins with rapidly down-dropping jaw ;
" You'll wonder perhaps how I came to be there ? "
" Not at all ! " he responded, " I really don't care ! "

'Twas scarcely a time to feel sympathetic
  With your legs all exposed to the midnight air ;
Humanity's not over-peripatetic
  At that witching hour with its legs all bare !
And Nuggins felt desperate—" No, its no sham ;
  For your body," he shouted, "I don't care a damn!"

The ghost gave a start, then clutched at our friend
  And caught him once more in his powerful grasp,
" I won't "—he hissed out—"I do not intend
  " To relax my hold—your arm I shall clasp

" Till you promise to bring yonder body to land

" And bury it decently—swear, hand in hand ! "

" In life my name was Timothy Juggins

  " And I used to be remarkably merry

" From morning to night "—"dear me ! " quoth Nuggins,

  " That sounds uncommonly odd—yes, very—

" I mean for a ghost "—he said apologetically

For once in a way feeling quite sympathetically.

" I was walking this spot a week now ago

  " When there crept up behind me a cursed sneaking hound

" Who dealt me, right here, a terrible blow

  " That scattered my brains all over the ground,

" Then into the pool he cast my poor frame "—

Even Nuggins was touched and said, " What a shame ! "

" Be a man ! " cried the ghost, " and take now the plunge ! "

  " What ! now ! " chattered Nuggins—" goodness me !
    Not for Joe !

" I might as well chuck the whole blooming sponge

  " As into that icy cold water go ;

" Its all very well for a bony old ghost,
" Who has no flesh upon him to freeze or to roast ! "

" And really I can't linger here any longer
   To argue the point "—but the ghost cried, "You must ! "
" I know," Nuggins went on; " that you are the stronger
   " And could pound my body to jelly or dust,
·· But you mustn't invite me just now to a swim
" If you really would like me to bury *him* ! "

And Nuggins looked out on the water cold,
   And then at that floating, shapeless thing,
At the best of times he wasn't too bold
   And now he felt—well—something less than a king ;
Besides, that thing might have been a dead cat,
And he wasn't inclined for a ducking for that !

Then an icy cold blast came and tickled his feet—
   When all of a sudden he woke with a scream ;
" Good gracious ; why—what's become of my sheet
   " And my blankets ! oh ! What a horrible dream !
" I declare I've tumbled clean out of my bed
" And am lying upon the cold boards instead ! "

And then he remembered that to some Welsh rare-l
　He'd greedily helped himself largely that night—
Its a way that it has—I may say a bad habit—
　To rend an inordinate large appetite;
But Nuggins was thankful to find that the ghost
Was only the whim of a " rabbit " at most.

When Snaggs, who was not in the humour for sleeping,
Stole out of his room, on tiptoe creeping,
Having, as he went down, slipped on his old gown,
Desirous of seeking some book to peruse
Or evening paper that had the last news,
Which, having annexed, without being caught,
He returned to the room he had left, *as he thought*,
And sank, all unheeding the woes that befall men,
In the big armchair that was built for your tall men,
Serenely contented and peaceful with all men.

He was deeply immersed in some city transaction,
His face brimming over with smug satisfaction,
When the door gave a creak and in walked a lady,
Her hair crimped with curls, and, the room being shady,
She did not observe that it boasted a tenant
Or that Mr. Snaggs had hoisted his pennant
On the back of the door in the shape of his breeches—
Sure sign of the sex—heaven knows what her screeches
Might have been had she happened to notice behind her
Of a poor man's requirements so stern a reminder!

Mr. Snaggs turned pale and then turned red,
Then convulsively clutched at the clothes of the bed,
As the lady began to exchange with her glass
Those looks that in private we're tempted to pass ;
Then taking a glance at his own *deshabille*
And beginning in turn hot and cold fits to feel
And scared at the thought of revealing himself
In such a predicament—what wicked elf
Could have led him to make such a wretched mistake,
Which he quickly found when he looked around !—
Without hesitation or pausing to think,
Or stopping to rest on uncertainty's brink,
Or giving himself but a moment to wink,
He gently slid from out the chair,
   The lady's back being turned to him,
And wishing himself—well—anywhere
   Except where he was !—though he wasn't slim,
He deftly rolled himself under the bed,
And lay like a mouse or as mummy as dead
At the moment the lady was rustling her papers
And prevented from hearing him cutting his capers.

Thus safely esconsced Snaggs began to surmise
What a fool he'd been not to risk a scene
In spite of the lady's possible cries—
But 'twas too late now ; perforce he must stay
Till sleep on the lady's eyelids lay ;
What cannot be cured must just be endured,
But supposing the lady should spy his !—that
Was a danger of course, and there his cravat
Lay flat on the table right under her nose,
But still he must wait till the danger arose—
So far he was safe, and that was the main thing,
And as for his fears, it was only a vain thing
This and that to conjecture—he hoped that the lady
Would just hurry up and come to the aid he
Required by tucking herself into bed
And snoring as if she'd a cold in the head.

So he lay on the boards as hard as a bunk
Like a rat in a trap and a pretty good funk,
And all he could see from under the bed
Was a pair of slim ankles that seemed highly bred ;

'Twas a poor consolation I frankly admit,
But not every man on so dainty a bit
Of a lady's attractions is able to feast
Without annoying their owner the least;
As a rule their garments hide all they can
From the too prying gaze of inquisitive man.

Poor Jonathan Snaggs! How theory fades
When practice the lighter domain invades!
For under the bed was a fine upper crust
Of misplaced matter that's known as dust,
Which is apt to make one's olfactories itch,
And when that happens, as a rule that which
Relieves the pressure, to wit, a sneeze
Follows quick in its train; and now to freeze
And sweat alternately Snaggs began;
While his blood froze up the water ran
In rivulets over his haggard face
As he felt that sneeze was gathering pace—
Alas and alas! for, strive as he might
To check his foe in the act of its flight,

It came at length as from a volcano
Like a healthy burst *e corpore sano—*
Oh! how his heart thumped as he heard the panes rattle,
'Twas like the first shot in a coming battle!

The lady startled immediately grasped
The situation and fairly gasped,
As from under the bed a leg she espied
Advancing forth, and while she cried
" Murder" and "help," she seized the tongs
And began to rattle its steely prongs
Across Snaggs' shins, which he gladly withdrew
Under cover again and kept from view;
But in no way inclined to be balked of her prey
As a well-trained dog keeps a stag at bay,
The lady dashed at them under the bed
And struck at his ribs, his back and his head,
Till Snaggs in his turn cried "murder" and "help"
In a voice half between a sob and a yelp,
And the other inmates, hearing the pother,
Rushed breathlessly in one after the other,
And called to the lady in frantic flurry

JONATHAN SNAGGS

" What on earth is the meaning of all this scurry ?
As she clattered the tongs with might and main
In and out, in and out, again and again—
" It's a burglar ! " she cried, as they stood appalled
" I'm not a burglar ! " Snaggs faintly called,
But no one heard him amidst the din
And clamorous state the lady was in—
" Pull him out, get hold of him, seize him tight ! "
But none seemed inclined the advice to mind,

   For they all of them stood in an abject fright,
Though the inoffending valance to rags
They tore in pretending to get at poor Snaggs !
At last came the butler, and he more bold
Of one of our Jonathan's legs got hold,
Then they all lent a hand and grasping it tight
They hauled the poor fellow out into the light,
All covered with dust and confusion, and hot,
At which they cried out in amazement—" What !
Jonathan Snaggs ! No, no ! Is it him ? "
To which he replied in a sally grim,
" I've heard of a *mauvais quart d'heure* before,

But to spend fifteen minutes on that beastly floor,
To be beaten and poked at till "black and blue"
But faintly describes my colour and hue—
" 'Tis all a mistake ! "—And then he narrated,
As he puff'd and panted, how he had been fated,
His dressing-gown swaying like Senator's robes
And his eyes starting forth like an orator's globes ;
But whether his audience wholly believed
What he told them or held that they might be deceived
I'm unable to say ; but suffice it to state
He went off next day at a quarter to eight,
And that one of the guests who wasn't a talker
Put his thumb to his nose as though to say, "Walker!"
But the lady forgave him—that I can state,
For she's now Mrs. Snaggs I'm glad to relate,
And she hasn't, I'm told, regretted her fate !

BETSY GRIG

Betsy Grig was an elderly maid,
Thin and angular, steady and staid,
Though by the aid of art and skill,
A wig at the back, in front a frill,
Cosmetics and dyes, laid on with a brush,
A set of false teeth, and a pair of—hush !
I mustn't be prying below the face ;
Suffice it to state that for figure and grace
She stood pretty well in the foremost flight
A little way off with her back to the light,
For the highest art it is to conceal
The ravages Nature is sure to reveal,
When once old Time has set his seal.

The story it falls to my lot to relate
Was spun one day by an adverse fate ;

And scorning the use of any half measures
Possess them of all those dearly-loved treasures.

So these lads might be seen about one of the clock
Most cautiously trying the bedroom lock;
But first they listened and heard a snore
Which hap'ly concealed the creak of the door
As they stealthily turned its well-polished handle
And found to their joy a dim night-candle
Just blinking in one of a pair of soap-dishes,
Which helped them to gain the tip-top of their wishes.
Then they silently crept on hands and knees
To the measured time of the burbling breeze
That was coming in puffs from under the frieze;
And they stole along till they came to the hose
And lit on a pair—yes, a pair of those—
But I mustn't forget my promise and so
I will pass them by—then they found a row
Of pearls that looked like the human tusk—
But you mustn't forget it was only dusk—
And they rifled the table whereon lay the hair,
Whose gloss helped to make our Betsy so fair,

And secretly the rosy heap
  I smuggled to my study,
To share them with an Irish boy
  Whose name was Jack McCuddy.

Now apples have, as all men know,
  A permeating scent,
And 'twas the Master's nose revealed
  The spot to which they went;

I well remember at the time
  I thought it was a chouse
That like a terrier he should go
  And sniff about the house;

And then he sought another spot—
  My skin still smarts and itches !—
As *he* took down his birch, while *I*
  Alas! took down my breeches;

And then he gave me what in fun
  He called " a stern reminder,"

And certainly the well-plied birch
  Left several marks behind her.

And I was left—well, truthfully
  I wasn't quite "left sitting,"
For as I couldn't sit that day
  The phrase would not be fitting.

But let me tell you this, my friends,
  A birching's not all woe ;
It leaves behind—just try it once—
  A splendid after-glow.

And then your pals will all come up
  And gently sympathise ;
By drawing long you're sure to be
  A hero in their eyes.

But what rejoiced me more than all,
  The innocent McCuddy
Received a dozen strokes or so
  Because his boots were muddy.

So then perhaps you'll all agree
   That school's a happy time ;
At any rate you won't refuse
   To applaud my simple rhyme.

And when the day is extra cold,
   Instead of mixing toddy,
Apply the birch—its sure to bring
   A glow into your body !

THE CYNIC

The cynic sat back in his snug armchair
And gazed at the fire with a stony stare;
He was cross and peevish and glum that night
And each red coal had the look of a sprite;
His spectacles blue wore a sombre hue
And nothing seemed proper, correct or true;
The world was travelling upside down,
And his butler, he vowed, was a clumsy clown;
His lawyer, he muttered, was grasping and crafty,
The weather was vile and the whole house was draughty
The prim housemaid's shoes were as noisy as clamps,
The Stock Exchange worse than an eyrie of scamps;
The sun the whole day had looked horribly bilious,
And made him feel down in his luck—supercilious—
Beyond what was usual—but not to confuse you all,
I will merely add that the world seemed askew,
And as much out of joint as the knees of a screw.

All at once our cynic dosed off in a dream

And snored like a steam-engine letting off steam ;

He dreamt that Old Nick from the cinders arose

And snatching the tongs had tweaked off his nose ;

He dreamt that his tailor had come with his shears,

And, to pay his account, had snipped off his ears ;

That the barber, whose gossip had made his brain spin,

Had razor'd his head instead of his chin ;

He dreamt that the doctor had cut off his tongue,

And with a long knife had removed his right lung ;

While, as for the dentist, he'd frightened him so,

That his teeth fell out of his mouth in a row ;

So that, when he awoke with a start and a fright,

Like a man who has put up a ghost in the night,

He rushed to the glass with a flaming light

To see how he looked, and was much relieved

When he saw his old face, though a trifle paler,

Like a man who is just from hanging reprieved,

And for once in a way shakes hands with his jailer.

'Tis curious to note how trifling a thing

Will check the pendulum in its swing ;

And dyes and cosmetics—the drawers they ransacked then
And into their pockets the treasures they packed them,
And carried away like a pair of jackdaws
Whatever, in short, came into their claws.

Poor Betsy! Next morn, what a guy she looked
With the deep lines of creases all rugged and crooked!
Ah! little she knew that her goose was cooked,
When she gazed on her bosom now minus its stuffing,
And her hair that was sadly in need of its puffing,
With a round white patch, showing bare of its thatch,
Like a sleek priest's tonsure that is made to match
The comb of a coot—and her angular form
Like the stump of a tree snapped off in a storm;
But what did it matter? " Ah! don't I possess,"
She muttered, " the aids that will win a caress ? "
Then she searched on the table, but—my goodness
    gracious !—
'Twas bare of her needs, though roomy and spacious;
Then she looked for her—yes—her dear " toosipegs,"
As she tenderly called them; but, oh! for her legs!
How they quivered and shook when she found no trace

Of those shining pearls to set off her face!
Then she turned in dismay to look—well, for that,
That did duty for what in its absence was flat,
And when she discovered that it, too, was gone,
And she of the whole of her treasures was shorn,
Her face turned as white as the ghostly moon
And she gave a loud shriek and fell in a swoon.

Then out flew the guests and hurriedly rushed
As fast as they could with their faces all flushed
To find—well, they stared in the direst confusion,
Half-inclined to apologise for their intrusion,
For, in place of the well-conditioned Miss Grig,
Here lay an old lady minus her wig
And minus her teeth and minus the dyes
That smothered her face right up to her eyes,
And minus—but there! suffice it to say
That as flat as a well-flattened pancake she lay;
And had it not been for her nose and her dress
'Tis not à far-fetched supposition to guess,
However the fact may be hard to believe,
They wouldn't have known Miss Betsy from Eve;

And one and all cried, as they stood around flocking

In chorus, " Dear me ! dear me ! how shocking ! "

And almost neglected her serious faint

At finding how much she owed to her paint ;

But they picked Betsy up and put her to bed

And sent for the doctor to have her bled,

Then fell tooth and nail to picking to pieces

The face that was left with nothing but creases,

Which they did, it is safe to infer, *con amore ;*

But here I must bring to a finish my story,

For narrating the clamour and fuss that arose

From the very beginning right up to the close

Would be like a broad stream that eternally flows.

HAPPY SCHOOLDAYS

Old fogies say that schooldays are
   The happiest time of life—
I haven't dared to hint as much
   To the lady who's my wife!

But I'll narrate an incident
   To illustrate the same,
That happened at the school where I
   Was up to every game.

Outside the master's garden stood
   Of apple trees a pair;
Of course the trees were out of bounds
   As all the nice things were;

And that the fruit was coveted
   You will perhaps believe;

HAPPY SCHOOLDAYS

Where is the boy who willingly
    Would not have followed Eve ?

For Eve it was in that regard
    Who first man's honour smirched,
And many a boy for that same crime
    Has since been soundly birched.

Now what a parlous state of things !—
    But as the task he grapples
The sweetest problem each boy tried
    Was how to steal those apples.

So as the clock struck four one morn
    I stole from out the house,
Making no sound, as though I were
    A well-conducted mouse ;

And while the sun was scarce awake
    And couldn't carry tales,
I'd picked enough from off those trees
    To fill a dozen pails.

From dreaming how dismal the world might be
Our cynic was greatly refreshed to see
That it really wore a much sweeter complexion ;
All at once there ensued a complete resurrection ;
Instead of its being all shadows and shades,
A long steep ascent without any grades,
He arose half inclined to kiss all the maids
And skip round the room, had not Dame Propriety
Enjoined a little more seemly sobriety.
But the Hall which had lived in the depths of the dumps
Had all of a sudden a fit of the jumps,
Which frightened to death the whole army of frumps
There were parties and balls and neighbourly calls,
Gymkanas and races in all sorts of places
And dinners and suppers for servants and "uppers,"
Till all the world wondered midst plaudits that thundered
What on earth could have come to their cynical neighbour
Who life was now one prolonged blast on the tabor.

But with all his proclivity towards joyous festivity
Our cynic still flouted the feminine gender,
Whether stolid and short or sprightly and slender ;

Not a single fair dame could create an impression
Though many a one had schemed for possession
Of a name and fortune and handsome estate
Which seemed an almost irresistible bait ;
But however polite from morning to night
He seemed disinclined to share his fat patrimony
With the pleasures or pains that accompany matrimony.

But meddlesome fate when unkindly inclined
In its clogs will our humble humanity bind ;
For going one night too early to bed
Another bad dream slipped into his head.
He dreamt that he'd lived to a doddering age
Beyond the last stage prescribed by our sage ;
And beyond the brief space allowed by the Psalmist
Who has shown himself now to be an alarmist,
And the picture he saw was a palsied old man
On the trembling brink of his life's last span
With no loving friend his last moments to tend
Or hold the thin hand when approaching the end ;
With all his affairs in the hands of a scamp
And at his bedside a drunken old " Gamp ; "

He heard her loud snore, he smelt the strong brandy
That she always kept near in a teacup so handy ;
He felt himself in her rough hands well shaken
Like a bottle of medicine sent to be taken ;
While worse than all this her drunken caresses—
Necessity drives when his Lordship possesses—
He had to submit to—alas ! what a fate
For a man with a fortune and landed estate !

It was only a dream, but he jumped up in haste
The very next morn not a moment to waste
And to wash from his mouth so unpleasant a taste,
And he strode straight away to the first girl he met,
Who has hardly subdued her astonishment yet,
And popped that old question so very momentous,
And for good or for evil extremely portentous ;
And though it was nearly as much of a shock
As a pretty stiff sentence to one in the dock,
The girl isn't born—at least there arn't many
Who'd reject such an offer, I'll wager a penny ;
And though 'tis good strategy just to refuse,
That is only, you know, a sort of a ruse ;

And the day hadn't gone so very far "forrard"
Nor the sun turned round on its road to the nor'ard,
Before they were kissing and twining their fingers
In a way around which fond memory lingers.

Oh! what a grand sight and what a delight
Were the wedding and ball that took place at the hall!
There were Prince Paraquete with the whole of his suite
And Lord Snuffanuffy, so stern and so huffy,
With his daughter all smiles and dimpled and bonny
Which quite won the heart of the tall lanky "Johnny"
Who, though in the Guards, had been ruined at cards,—
But not being dyspeptic of rumours I'm sceptic—
And Baronets two with their daughters in blue
And a mother-in-law in a deuce of a stew;
There were nice boys and girls all flirting of course
And a jilted young swain who looked peevish and cross—
There stood the old Bishop in brand-new gaiters
And a dozen or two of ghostlike waiters,
There was lean Mr. Lisp and little Miss Mincing
Who thought the dear Bishop so very convincing,
While not very far away sat Mrs. Plump,

Whose husband of course was as straight as a pump,
For things in this world have an opposite trend,
Though they work out all right, I suppose, in the end.

At last when the crackers had all been exploded
And brim-high the whole of the glasses were loaded,
The Bishop arose with a rubicund face,
Not to preach them a sermon nor yet to say grace,
But to offer the toast of the day in their place :
" This is, my dear friends, a most solemn occasion,"
Said his Lordship in tones of the deepest persuasion ;
" Our two young friends for better or worse
" Are now tied as tight as the strings of my purse."
" Hear, hear ! " cried Miss Mincing, without any
wincing,
" What a splendid simile ! " cried her little friend,
Jimmy Lee.
" ' Tis a bit of a plunge," the Bishop went on,
" When the wedding garment we suddenly don ;
" But, my friends, I know you'll agree with me
" That in this case it fits our friends to a T.
" 'Tis a magical shirt when its properly fitted,

" And the wearers are not in the least to be pitied."
" Hear, hear ! " burst forth as the glasses chinked
And the Bishop and host at each other winked;
" So, now that the knot is thus happily tied,
" I ask you to drink to the bridegroom and bride
" With thrice three cheers, hurrah and hurrah !
" And may some one soon call them papa and mamma ! "

Our cynic no longer was troubled with dreams,
But whether it was the strawberry creams
Or the iced champagne that got into her head,
That night, when Miss Mincing climbed into her bed,
She began to dream the most terrible scene
That in all this world could ever have been—
For old Nick and his crew had appeared at the wedding
And just as the guests a few teardrops were shedding,
Which I must endorse " crocodilish " in source,
Old Nick started from an invisible place
And indulged in a most repulsive grimace;
The glasses he swept with a flick of his tail,
And the guests he dispersed with a sweep of his flail ;

The Bishop he hoisted as high as the roof
With a well-placed kick from his cloven hoof,
While the Prince and his suite old Nick and his merry "Co."
Despatched somewhere to the region of Jericho;
Indeed they were scattered so far into space
That none of them ever returned to their place;
And as for the others, my Lord Snuffanuffy,
Who had grown by high living exceedingly puffy,
Was a sort of football to old Nick in the hall,
Who kept the old man so long on the bounce
That he lost every single superfluous ounce;
Indeed such a scene could never have been;
But the bridegroom and bride to the hour that they died
At the poor woman's tale used to laugh till they cried,
And old Nick and his crew ever after defied.

THE RECTOR AND THE PARROT

'Twas a Sabbath morn on which the plot
Of my tale is laid; the actual spot
Was an east coast village that depended on tillage
And voted free trade the most scandalous pillage,
In the centre of which a farmhouse stood
To the south of a closely-knitted wood,
Where sounded that morning a grand alarm
That ran through the length and breadth of the farm,
For the farmer, his wife, his daughters and all
The lesser lights of the servants' hall
Were rushing about to try and discover
Their pet grey parrot, who, like a lover,
Had escaped from her domicile, courting a scene,
And, for aught they knew, was at Gretna Green;
So they all set to work and hunted the house
From cellar to garret for poor polly parrot;

They peeped in the larder where hung the prized grouse
Just sent by the squire from some northern shire ;
They ran through the gardens, examined the pond,
They hunted the beds and the bushes beyond,
They climbed up the roof, they shook all the trees,
They called and they shouted, till all by degrees
Arrived at the fact that polly was gone,
An untimely beginning to that Sabbath morn.

The Reverend Charles Theophilus Grundy
Was moodily walking to church that Sunday ;
He was not over popular with his parishioners,
Who found him, when claiming his aid as petitioners,
As kindly disposed as your taxing commissioners ;
Yet his church was crowded by way of a treat
From the top to the bottom with all the *élite*
As well as more humbly-clad men of the street ;
For the harvest thanksgiving announced for that day
Had called up a quite unaccustomed display,
And Hodge and has wife helped to made up the show,
And landlords and tenants all knelt in a row,
Though why they were there I'm sure I don't know,

Unless 'twas to pray that the corn might boom a bit,
For all they could make was nine shillings a coomb of it.

The service went smoothly until at the close
Of the Creed a wild scene of confusion arose ;
For the words had scarcely concluded—when
From the rafters there sounded a solemn " Amen,"
Which through the whole congregation rang
And made the old clerk drop his book with a bang,
While the people from smiling could scarcely refrain—
Indeed they renewed it again and again
As after each prayer that solemn " Amen "
Now loud, now soft, resounded aloft,
Till some of the weaker conjectured Old Nick
Himself had descended to play them a trick,
For, crane as they might, 'twas as dark as the night
At the pitch of the roof whence came the response
That deprived the old clerk of his wits for the nonce.

My friends, you'll have guessed who the culprit was
Without my having to tell you, because
'Tis as plain as any long-winded digression ;

But perhaps I may make a little concession
In order to put you in proper possession
Of all the points in this very weird case ;
These parrots, you know, are a very strange race,
Renowned for their powers of quaint imitation,
Unwonted discernment and shrewd contemplation !
And sometimes the nautical speech of a sailor,
Which differs from that of our Jeremy Taylor,
They are known to affect, and 'twas this dialect
Our parrot had learnt to so great a perfection
That she knew how to speak without fear of detection.
Moreover, this bird knew all things in their season
And seemed to be blest with the highest of reason ;
She knew when to say " good morning and night,"
She knew all the household by name and by sight,
And the language she'd use whenever she chose
To loosen her tongue is just one of those
Improprieties greater than I dare disclose.

Now, had these " Amens" concluded the whole
Of Polly's wrong doing that morning, this scroll
Would not have been penned from beginning to end ;

But I'm sorry to state that when our grand Litany,
Which, as you well know, is intended to fit any
Or all of the troubles that man possesses
And save him from those entangled distresses
That hang round his march mid life's caresses—
When the people responded, " Good Lord, deliver us ! "
That breakfastless bird, who was feeling omnivorous,
Began to append her own adjuration
By screaming " Good Lord " to the consternation
Of the poor old Rector who thought that some man
Must have basely devised this dastardly plan
When Polly chimed in, concealed in her cavity,
While the people, unable to keep up their gravity
In spite of a scene of such awful depravity,
Nor yet to restrain dame nature's impulsions,
Were shaking their benches in heaving convulsions.

The poor old Rector suddenly stopped,
Then on to his feet with agility popped
As the bird right out his anathemas poured,
" You're a rogue ! you are ! " " Good Lord ! Good Lor
" My friends," said he, " I'm ashamed to think

That standing almost on eternity's brink
Such noises as these in hilarity drowned
Should within those sacred precincts resound ; "
And in speaking these words he frowned at the carls,
When at their conclusion, to his utter confusion,
A seductive voice whispered, " Come, kiss me, Charles !

The effect of this sally 'tis hard to pourtray ;
Effrontery seemed to be winning the day,
And the Rector looked over his " specs " in dismay
And applied his silk handkerchief straight to his face
To deaden the noise that was rising apace ;
For sublime and ridiculous seemed to have met
Within that sacred edifice, yet
The poor man hardly dare credit his ears
For one cannot believe the half that one hears ;
But, at length, his cup being filled to the brim
He announced that, after singing a hymn,
The service would close, being anxious to end
A scene he himself was unable to mend.
He chose the Old Hundredth, that popular rhyme,
T is heartily rendered in every clime

And is bound to endure to the end of old time ;
But here the climax was suddenly reached,
For that ill-mannered bird set to work and screeched
At the highest pitch of her well-charged lungs,
Like a scolding virago with six or eight tongues,
A famous old song, which, mixed with the hymn,
Made a medley that sounded uncommonly grim.
Then arose a scene of the wildest confusion,
For the service was brought to a hasty conclusion,
And the Rector unable to stand the strain
Of the blasphemous riot that rang through the fane
To the vestry rushed off, like a shot from a cannon,
While that mischievous bird still laughingly ran on
The same old tune that she'd picked up aboardship—
I wonder what would have occurred, had his Lordship,
The pompous old Bishop, been present to witness
A scene that reversed all one's notions of fitness.

Then the Rector fled forth from the church with a gait
As swift as the the rush of a gathering spate,
His garments all streaming, his head in a swirl,
Spinning round and round in resistless whirl,

And sat himself down with a terrible frown
To write to the Bishop resigning his living—
The finishing touch to that hearty thanksgiving ;
And many the jest and many the smile
That herald the story of poor Polly's guile,
As the village folk sit at the cottage door
Rehearsing the deeds of that day o'er and o'er
And wishing to goodness she'd given them more.

TOM BROWN *

1.

Old Tom was a salt that lived by the shore
  Near the fortified town of Dover,
And his heart so rejoiced to *sail* over *the seas*
  That he *sailed* more than *half-seas-over ;*
For he kept some fine *ale* and *good spirits* on *sale*
  At a tavern yclept the " What cheer ! "
Yet he constantly dreamt, for his sins no doubt,
That *bad spirits* were chasing him, in and out,
  And feasting upon his *bier.*

2.

And the *rum* that he loved his friends christened
  ' *Brown Tom,*'
  For why ? it upset *Tom Brown ;*

---

* I desire to claim no originality for any of the puns here
perpetrated. Previous writers, particularly Tom Hood, have
almost exhausted the English language in this respect, but
I have not intentionally borrowed from them.—R.

But, whatever he took, there was always some spoo
  That followed him up dale and down ;
And *spirits* within and *spirits* without,
  Spirits in dark and in light,
'Twas a *rum* sort of go such a *spirited* show
Should seize on a man whose *spirits* were low,
  And turn to *a-gobblin'* by night.

3.

But one morning a stave by his missus' grave
  He *sharply* set out for to sing,
And though he sang *flat*, he couldn't help that,
  It was such a *natural* thing ;
When out of the womb of each blessèd tomb
  The *shade* of its inmate arose,
And sat on its mound with its feet on the ground
Without so much as the *ghost* of a sound,
  Nor yet with a vestige of hose.

4.

He thought of eternity's *razor*-like *edge*,
  As he murmured, " By Jove, what a *shave !* "

When he suddenly tripped, as his shaky foot slipped
  On the *edge* of a newly-dug grave ;
And he fell with a flop right on to the top
  Of a coffin but freshly deposited ;
Like a *shell newly-laid* it burst with a pop,
While his breath was knocked out, and his heart gave a stop,
For he'd scarcely been used to so stiffish a *drop*
  Nor with *spirits* so closely encloseted.

5.

'Twas not, after all, the *Judgement day*,
  Though his *day of Judgement* was near,
For his spirit was laid by the sexton's spade,
  As he whistled a tune o'er his *beer ;*
And though he screamed out with a frantic shout
  The digger was deaf as a hearse ;
But that, you must know, was the *rummiest* go
When his body was tied to a *spirit* below,
  For better, it may be—or worse.

6.

And that was the end of the poor *clod*, Brown !
  He quickly became a *brown clod*,

Though his poor body, shrunk with the *ether* he'd drunk,
　　Must have formed an *ethereal* sod ;
And his friends held *a wake*, while his dead body *slept*,
　　And mournfully set up the *wine ;*
But some at his death were *mightily* glad,
For the *maggots* a right royal feast must have had
　　When they met on *old Tom* to dine.

MORAL.

If you want to keep *up good spirits*, don't put
　　Such a host of *bad spirits down*,
For *gin* is a *snare*, and of *rum* beware,
　　It's a *queer* effect on the crown ;
And remember that when your *spirits* are *low*,
　　Other *spirits* are sure to jump *up*,
And, though very *thin*, they apt to come *thick*,
And you're certain to see the face of old Nick
　　Grinning out of the dearly-loved cup.

SIMPKINS' BED

Friend Simpkins was nervous, of that there's no doubt,
The bray of an ass turned him inside out,
While the thought of a ghost, such a fright was he in,
Was sufficient to make him jump out of his skin,
Which is needful to state lest what I relate
Should make people think I've invoked pure invention,
Which I vow is removed very far from intention;
No! my story is true, at least I've been told so,
And I doubt if it's one that invention could mould so.

Now Simpkins one day received a request
From a very old friend, and of sportsmen the best,
To pack up his things and run down for a shoot,
And being so friendly he added, to boot,
He might have to turn out his coachman or groom,
Though he wasn't quite sure he could give him a room,

But a "shake-down" he'd find of some sort or kind,
And the shoot being one to Simpkins' mind,
For of pheasants he knew that last year they slew
A thousand or more and rabbits galore,
And he wouldn't have missed it for all he was worth
With the added enjoyment to which it gave birth,—
He accepted at once and flew on time's wings—
For a train, as we know, cannot boast of such things—
But I speak, I need hardly aver, metaphorically,
Though my tale may itself be accepted historically.

Arrived at his journey's end, Simpkins soon found
That the house had been crammed from attic to ground,
And his friend, the kind host, with ample apology,
And language that cannot be traced to theology,
Was obliged to admit that, though he might sit,
Which was better than standing, there wasn't a bed
Upon which his friend Simpkins could lay his poor head ;
But necessity driving when other expedients
Have failed to supply the proper ingredients,
And scratching his head to help out his plan,
The well-known resort of idealess man,

He suggested with all the *applon* he was able
That a capital bed the dining-room table
Would make when the dishes were put out of sight
And Simpkins was on it laid out for the night.

There is nothing to do upon such an occasion
But to pat your host's back as though the invasion
Were partly your own imperfect contrivance
Or at any rate done with your ready connivance,
And accept it with all the possible grace
Without so much as a shrug or grimace.
So Simpkins that night for once found himself
Tucked up on the table, as if on a shelf,
Though indeed it was worse, if his woes I rehearse;
A tumble is imminent from either side,
While the surface is equally bad for your hide;
For the wood is so hard you cannot but shift
Every minute or so, and your carcase you'll lift
To find a fresh spot that is free from the ache
You are certain to feel if you still are awake,
While slumber is almost out of the question,
However so tired, or good your digestion,

And you're like, should you rashly give way to sleep,
To find yourself cast on the floor in a heap.

It was just when poor Simpkins was sleepless and restless
And wishing to goodness the table were guestless,
That he heard to his horror a creak of the door,
And as the moon cast a dim light on the floor,
He saw what he knew full well was a ghost
Glide up to the table as prim as a post ;
Not daring to breathe, or murmur aloud,
He saw the ghost lay what he felt was his shroud
Right over him, carefully smoothing it out—
He was far too nervous to remonstrate or shout—
Then upon it he felt that unearthly ghost lay
In quite an adept and methodical way
At intervals regular, neat and precise
With a clang that betokened things other than mice,
A number of hard and tangible articles,
And, though each was light, such a number of particles
Became quite oppressive when all were laid out,
To complete which transaction a bottle a stout

The ghost polished off, having first drawn the cork
In a professional way with the aid of a fork.

Believing at length in the ghost's disappearance,
And feeling assured he'd effected a clearance,
Friend Simpkins peeped out, then swiftly arose
As he cast to the ground the whole of his clothes,
When to his dismay there ensued such a rattle
As might have occurred in the din of a battle,
For a hundred articles fell to the ground
And made such a clashing and terrible sound
That his wits, which had previously strayed just a little,
Quite left him—at least they left not a tittle
Of reason behind them, for Simpkins dashed out
Of the room that had been the scene of the rout
And tumbled right into the arms of his host,
Who thought in his turn he was clutching a ghost
And began to belabour his terrified guest
Until, as he afterwards said, he was blest
If he knew whether on his own legs he was standing
In the heat of the fray at the top of the landing.

I daresay, my friends, you have heard folks talking
Of things done by men when in their sleep walking.
I remember the case of a man who was found
Perambulating his garden around,
Having only upon him his *chemise de nuit*,
And when asked if he didn't feel—just a wee
Bit cold, he replied by lifting his shirt
Straight up from behind, and with action alert
Enfolding it round his neck as he said,
" You see I've a shawl to wrap round my head ! "
Forgetting that now his body was bare ;
I wish Mrs. Grundy herself had been there,
I venture to think 'twould have caused her to stare,
And if she had stared, unless I am dreaming,
The fussy old girl would have killed herself screaming.

But though you'll partly have guessed Simpkins' history,
'Tis my task to unravel the whole of the mystery.
The Butler was wont to walk in his sleep
Every night, I'm told, and when slumbers deep
With snores more or less, as the case may be,

Had sealed the eyes of the inmates, he
Would arise and by force of habit lay
The table with unaccustomed display
So neat and exact as reality passes
With knives, spoons and forks and dishes and glasses ;
And on this occasion no note he took
That Simpkins might haply take him for a spook ;
Indeed he never took heed of the fact
That a guest in the shape of poor Simpkins was packed
'Twixt sheets on the table—he set to work
With a right good will and bustle and smirk
To balance the items from head to toe
Just as if there was nought but a table below ;
And so, my friends, you can guess without mockery
What a crash must have come when the whole of the
    crockery
Was launched on the floor as Simpkins arose
In the dead of the night and cast off the bedclothes.

I needn't enlarge on the host's expressions
Of deepest regret, or the Butler's confessions,

THE SLEEPWALKER AND THE MISSIONARY

Traditions that cling round our mansions manorial
With antiquity flavoured from time immemorial
Have a claim to respect, and therefore I beg
You'll listen to those of Miss Dorothy Wegg,
Who, had she a knot that needed untying,
Her furthermost efforts completely defying,
Had only to wait till sleep held her tight
And she lay in the arms of somniferous night,
When certain it is that, as soon as the light
Of the sun's fierce ray had emblazon'd the day,
She would find it undone in a marvellous way.

For instance, I give you just one little fact
That borders upon supernatural act
And cannot be sniffingly poohed by agnostics—
If unable to do some tormenting acrostics,

She'd quietly place them under her pillow,
And when she was soothingly rocked by the billow
Of sleep and as certain as eggs are eggs,
For the hand was undoubtedly Dorothy Wegg's,
She'd sit up in bed and there in the dead
Of night she'd unravel the tortuous skein
That had taxed her wits in the daytime in vain.

But lest you should think the possession of these
Supernatural gifts was certain to please,
It is my intention at this point to mention
That sometimes they sowed the seeds of dissension ;
As pitfalls surround the acts of our spooks
Her friends were for ever on sharp tenterhooks
For fear of what our Miss Wegg should do next,
Some portion of which is the cause of my text ;
But to show that the lady herself often came
To misfortune in playing so risky a game
An example I'll give illustrating the same :—
One night having dreamt that she was in prison
She found when she woke that she had arisen

And 'twixt the bars of a very black grate
Had succeeded in thrusting the whole of her pate;
Indeed it has often come into my mind
How odd she must have looked from behind;
But no one was present I'm glad to relate
The lady's condition exactly to state.

Yes! people who're prone to walk in the lone
Still night often find themselves in a sad plight
And sympathy joined to our laughter invite;
For instance, the man who hid his own trousers
And then made a stir like a dozen carousers
When his mutton-chopp'd valet came up in the morning-
Which led at once to his giving him warning—
Was not to be blamed, but more to be pitied,
For having to wear a strange-looking pair
That cannot be truthfully said to have fitted;
Indeed some might think him a theme for compassion
For having to wear what was out of the fashion.

So towards my sleep-bound peripatetic
I trust you're inclined to be sympathetic,

And, whether you live in the country or city,

You've room in your hearts for a morsel of pity.

It happened one day on a certain occasion

That a Parson of seemingly low-church persuasion

Had come to the village to give an address

On behalf of the blacks in some far wilderness.

Whether 'twas the society called the "Church Missionary,"

Whose aims always strike me as apt to be visionary—

I've noticed these clergymen sometimes outnumber

The whole of their scanty-clothed flock coloured umber—

I regret I forget—the point doesn't matter—

Or whether the niggers were Sikh or Mahratta,

Or Caffir or Zulu or in Honolulu,

'Tis wide of the point; to speak for the heathen

The Parson had travelled down from Innerleithen,

Each pocket containing a missionary box

In which to collect funds for buying some socks

Or clothing the blacks didn't keep on the stocks,

Which towards the end he gave out to our friend

In the hope they might prove a welcome receptacle

For the good folks' pence—too good to be sceptical—

And the Parson announced that, whatever the toil,
He'd return in a month to garner the spoil
And he hoped that his words would fall on good soil.

Now Miss Wegg—you must wait to see the connexion-
Had shining all round her face and complexion
A cluster of curls that were rightly the pride
Of the hair that was otherwise simply tied;
But what was her horror one very fine morn
On seeking her glass to find herself shorn
Of a dozen or so of these very dear pets;
'Twas like putting out a circle of jets
Of light in a single chandelier
That had formerly glittered so crystally clear.
At first she conjectured some rascally man
Must have boldly contrived this dastardly plan,
Or perhaps that some less well-adorned, jealous rival
Was guilty of this unworthy contrival
For robbing her thus of a part of the grace
That set off so well the rest of her face;
For, needless to say, "the rape of the lock"
She'd read in her youth and it gave her a shock—

Until she remembered another lock

Would intervene and come between

Herself and such a catastrophe

And that in that lock she had turned the key.

Then it flashed upon her that she herself

Must have been the cowardly, dastardly elf

Who had cut off the curls; but what had she done with
    them ?

Could her friends even now be having some fun with
    them ?

But look high and low, from the top to the bottom,

She couldn't conjecture who on earth could have got 'em

Or where she had put them—she hadn't a notion

And of course couldn't make a hue and commotion ;

So finding her search left her still in the lurch

She had to give up her endeavours to find them,

And as for her friends—she managed to blind them

By begging or buying from some other head

Fresh curls to shine in their place instead.

The Parson returns, as the twelvemonth ends,

The boxes to clear on behalf of his friends,

Which he'd left to Miss Dorothy Wegg to collect,

Who belonged to the same evangelical sect;

Arrived on the scene, with a flourish of trumpets

He first stood a tea with muffins and crumpets,

Then he opened the boxes, having rattled them first—

They were not inclined of their own weight to burst—

When he spied midst the pence and occasional shilling

What certainly was most uncommonly thrilling—

In each box lay a curl tied up with blue ribbon

As neat as a two-year-old babe with a bib on;

Miss Wegg raised her hands, as well she might,

To see her lost curls being dragged to the light,

While the Parson, whose face like a well-polished fork
shone,

Proceeded to put up her treasures to auction;

And Miss Wegg, as she afterwards said to her niece,

  Had the mortification to see her curls

Knocked down at an average twopence apiece

  To the huge delight of the village girls,

Who I think must have guessed whose head they'd
once crowned

By the smirks and the glances they signalled around.

'Twas fitting and right that Miss Wegg should pay
Our Parson out for that night's display ;
Though to one so refined it was far from her mind
To do aught but what was gentle and kind ;
But nevertheless it so fell out—
The Fates no doubt had brought it about—
For the Parson, who stayed at the mansion that night,
When every guest had put out his light,
Nor was heard in the house the stir of a mouse,
Was suddenly roused in a hideous fright
By feeling his blankets whipped off from his bed—
The poor man had a bad cold in the head—
And as he jumped up he'd only just time—
'Twas as good as a scene in a good pantomime—
A little retreating figure to spy
As it closed the door without wherefore or why,
And left him alone to shiver and pray
That the long cold night would soon turn into day.

To sound Miss Wegg's grief when she found out the
reason
The Parson next day kept his bed would be treason ;

And the fright she was in when she saw on her couch
A heap of strange blankets I dare not avouch ;
But the household I know were at sixes and seven
When they afterwards heard that this poor man of
　heaven
Had passed through the night in his own great coat,
As a friend of his some days afterwards wrote.
Well, it ended indeed as it should have begun,
A stop was at once put to this sort of fun,
And Miss Wegg, to hold her in bounds, has her keeper
Who is stated by nature to be a light sleeper ;
And when she mistakes her sleeping for waking
She has to submit to a moderate shaking,
Which is better than all this imbroglio-making.

THE BITER BIT

Sir William was rich and he lived in style
    At number 1, Chichester Square ;
No wife or children had he to beguile
    The hours that he passed alone there ;
The neighbours all called him " a cynical gent,"
Who grumbled and growled to the top of his bent.

Like spinsters and bachelors out of their youth
    Sir William had fads of his own ;
We can none of us help growing long in the tooth,
    But we needn't grow toothless alone ;
There are few of us worse for a little corrective,
And a spouse of our faults is the surest detective.

But of all his odd fads, what most had his scorn
    Was the keeping late hours of a night,
And a guest that came ringing at two in the morn
    Was sent straight about to the right ;

Indeed to gain entrance he might have to whistle,
For the servants daren't stir on pain of dismissal.

Now it happened one night about two of the clock
　　Sir William detected a noise ;
The thought of a burglar occasioned a shock,
　　As a rod to the toughest of boys ;
But it sounded as if it came from the ground,
Though 'tis hard to locate exactly a sound.

Sir William jumped up as he was in a trice
　　And groped his way down the front stairs,
As there scampered away from him beetles and mice
　　Whom he'd stumbled on all unawares ;
Then he fumbled his way to the steps of the area
As mute as a mouse in a trap—only warier.

But hesitate, listen and crane as he might,
　　Nought could he succeed in detecting ;
It was precious cold work at that time of night
　　To be standing there genuflecting
In a pretty keen draught and a suit of pyjamas,
Which is only done safely in stories and dramas.

Then he thought he would open the area door
  And step for a moment outside,
And he looked the whole area steps o'er and o'er
  As the organ of sight he applied,
When the door gave a bang and he found with dismay
That the lock was a patent and wouldn't give way.

'Twas an awkward predicament none can deny,
  The pavement was chilly as ice,
And the wind whistled round him both gusty and high
  In a way that was far from nice,
And Sir William's bald head grew cold as a stone,
And his flesh, which was portly, struck chill to the bone.

What was to be done ? If he shouted he knew
  Not a soul would come down to his aid ;
His orders would be—oh how the wind blew !—
  Observed by both butler and maid ;
He might ring, he might knock, he might whistle and shout,
Not a soul would care " tuppence " what it all was about.

Then a bobby came marching along with a tramp
  To warn all the world he was coming ;

'Tis hardly the way to capture a scamp
　　To make such a deuce of a humming;
I wonder the force is not *soled* with Scaithe's patent;
They'd be less often *sold* by lying more latent.

Sir William took cover inside the coal hole;
　　It was warmer against the *wall's end*,
And he couldn't well play in so scanty a rôle
　　To the force as he might to a friend;
So he stopped till the sound of the tramp-tramp had faded,
Though it left him an icycle, stiff and unaided.

What was to be done?　He couldn't stay there
　　Through the long and lonely night watching;
Could fortune, I wonder, have been well aware
　　What a nice little plot she was hatching?
Sir William next day, barrin' jokin' and scoffin',
If he didn't do something, would be in his coffin.

So he crept up the area steps and looked round,
　　And then at the windows he gazed;
They all looked as black, without giving a sound
　　As if they had never been glazed;

And he felt that his butler was snoring as though
A dozen trombones were blown in a row.

Yes ! there was his room right enough—happy thought !
  'Twas the end one upon the third floor ;
To throw with a cricket ball he'd been taught,
  And a stone lay close to the door ;
With a mighty effort—the action was rash—
He sent the stone bang through a pane with a crash !

A window-pane !—But, to his sorrow and shame,
  He saw that his aim was untrue,
For it crashed through a pane far removed from his aim
  Of the very next house—number 2 !
When up went the window and forth came a head
In nightcap and curls, newly risen from bed !

The cry of " Police " rang through the night air
  In shrieks successive and strong ;
In vain the poor man bade the shrieker forbear
  And cease her monotonous song ;
She couldn't be expected Sir William to know
In a suit of pyjamas all naked below.

Then the sole of the bobby was heard once again ;
   This time he came at a run ;
And Sir William rushed back to the cellar, for fain
   Would he such a degrading scene shun ;
How he shivered and shook !—he was dreadfully numb
And 'twas more than a chance to the cold he'd succumb.

But fate was his master.   The bobby, apprised
   Of the outrage so lately committed,
Began a strict search as the lady surmised—
   For she was keen-scented and witted—
That their object might be in the neighbouring cellar,
To which he replied he would look and then tell her.

Sir William was shaking like leaves in a storm
   When the door was flung rudely aside,
And a bull's-eye was turned on his quivering form,
   Which had once been of London the pride ;
And a voice bellowed forth—" Come hout of that there !
I see you, my man—resist if you dare ! "

And a truncheon was drawn and waved up and down
   In a horribly menacing way ;

Sir William in doubt put his hand to his crown
    As he stood like a lion at bay.
" Come hout of this, then, if you don't want a smasher,"
Roared the bobby, "come hout of this cellar, you
    masher ! "

The wit was not great, but I fear I must own
    Our friend cut a woe-be-gone figure,
For his flesh looked quite white, with the cold and the
    fright,
    While his suit was as black as a nigger ;
And to make matters worse the bobby had ripped
The seat of the garment that he'd roughly gripped.

Then in triumph to number 2 was he led
    To confront the irate one in curls ;
He couldn't say " boh to a goose," for his head
    Was in a tornado of whirls ;
And his tongue, which was always so mightily glib,
Seemed all of a sudden inclining to jib.

'Twas hard for a man in Sir William's position
    To confess to an action so shady,

Nor did it seem likely that any contrition
  Would succeed in appeasing the lady,
Unless he gave up—which he daren't—his right name,
For that would have covered him crimson with shame.

But the lady was sharper than one might suppose;
  She had studied her man in the light;
Indeed she had often admired his straight nose,
  His manner of dress and his height;
And though his pyjamas were black to the hem,
She could see quite enough of his figure through them.

And she wasn't herself wholly free from design,
  For she scented the odour of pelf,
And she would not allow that a bachelor fine
  Ought to spend the whole on himself;
So instead of the flaying Sir William expected,
A smile stealing over her face he detected.

Thus encouraged his tongue broke loose from its mooring
  And explained the bare simple fact,
To the policeman's chagrin who looked to be scoring
  For so prompt and successful an act,

And it ended, to make a long story short,
In the good lady towing Sir William to port.

But whether 'twas gratitude at the relief
   The lady so timely afforded,   .
Or whether it was that her person-in-chief
   With his heart and his feelings accorded,
'Tis sure there was never a grander affair
Than the wedding and ball in Chichester Square.

And Sir William has buried his fancies and fads;
   If you wish to stay out the whole night,
Or summon a meeting of prominent " Rads,"
   He will wring off your hand with delight;
For he's laid down a rule that what pleases a friend
Shall become the rule of his life to the end.

The moral of which is : Don't mope by yourself,
   But look out at once for a wife;
You'll find it, provided you're not short of pelf,
   The happiest change in your life;
And though you may happen to quarrel a bit,
If you're wise, 'tis on the box seat you will sit.

THE POODLE AND THE BRIAR

You ask me, dear Harry, to tune up my pipe
And let the poor partridges, pheasants and snipe
Be happy for once, while I sing you a song ;
Whether major or minor or short or long
You say doesn't matter a fig or a button,
Or whether I sing of ascetic, or glutton,
Or nasty Paul Pry, or your fiddling Nero,
Or back-slum scoundrel, or sixth-form hero—
I must somehow or other induce a smile ;
I'd better, I think, resort to some isle
Where old King Coal wears a brand-new tile ;
Though I'm rather inclined to alter my mind
And sing instead what comes into my head
Of men that are living or men that are dead ;
So my answer is—"All right ! Here goes !
I'll adjust my spectacles to my nose,

Forthwith buckle to, arrange my hose,
And for once as my own famous hero I'll pose !

'Twas a wet afternoon, I was feeling seedy,
Out of tune with the world, and of cash somewhat needy !
As I patiently sat in a "hard-class smoking"
With my clothes all wet, not to say all soaking,
And not in the least in the humour for joking,
When into the carriage a lady shuffled—
A lady I'll call her, her face being muffled—
Then looked around and sniffed and snuffled—
At least these sounds came from her direction,
But for company having no predilection
And to ladies' society a rooted objection,
"It's a smoker, Ma'am," I politely said,
Raising of course my hat from my head,
To which she merely replied with a sort
Of sound that appeared to resemble a snort ;
Then arranged her skirt, as much as to say,
"Smoking or not, here I mean to stay,"
Which I thought to myself was rather "bad form,"
But not wishing to raise in a teacup a storm,

I made up my mind those ills to endure
For the which mankind has provided no cure.

The train started off—we sat at each end
Of the carriage, when for my very dear friend,
The choicest piece of a well-coloured briar—
To what greater delight can a smoker aspire ?—
I began straight-away in my pockets to fumble
And said to myself with the shade of a grumble,
" I wonder if this good lady'll allow
Me to have a draw—I'll try anyhow"—
And I held my companion up to the light
By the open window—how polished and bright
My dear treasure looked—she was quite a picture !
You may try as much as you will to inflict your
Meerschaums on me—but here my thoughts
Were interrupted by sniffs and snorts,
As out from beneath the lady's skirt,
Where all the time he'd been snugly begirt,
A shock-headed poodle sprang with a bound,
And before I had time to speak or look round,

He'd dashed at my pipe—and in drawing it back

In the scrimmage it dropped from my hand—alack !

And out of the window it fell with a smack

Right on to the line and vanished from view—

Loved friend of my youth! "Then what did I do?"

I'll tell you, my boy; in less than a wink,

Before that blessed poodle had time to blink,

Or before I gave myself time to think

I'd picked him up by the scruff of his neck—

The little beast—and in less than a sec.,

Though the lady screamed shrill as an engine's whistl

And her claws went to work as sharp as a thistle,

Out went master poodle after my pipe

As swift as the flight of a well-fledged snipe,

With the train going quite thirty miles to the hour ;

Well !—that settled him ! No earthly power

Could have stayed my hand at the moment, but—

These horrid antitheses always will cut

Across the horizon—the deed being done

I had next to play at " consequences,"

Which somewhat took the edge off the fun,

For the lady went clean-bang out of her senses ;

She screamed and she wept—and I fancy she swore,
But I know that the next ten minutes or more
Proved to me an exceedingly *mauvais quart d'heure*,
If an Irishism's permissible—Sir,
Friend Harry, with all my breath I declare
It was like Hell let loose in the upper air
And confined within the space of my carriage,
And devoutly I blessed the sight of old Harwich,
When the train at last steamed into the station
And thus put an end to a strained situation.

But a grievous mistake, as it turned out, I made
In thinking we'd finished this slight escapade,
For the train had no sooner arrived, and stopped,
Than the lady sprang up, and out she popped,
And at once commenced to scream and to cry
At the top of her lungs—" guard, porter, hi !
" Police, police! here's a monster ! Come !
" Into custody take him ! " and midst the hum
Of gathering passengers, porters and guards
I was shuffled about like a pack of cards ;

In vain I tried to state the bare fact,
It was clear to them all I was caught in the act—
" He's murdered my pet—flung him out of the train,"
And her tears like a torrent 'gan freshly to rain
As this tune she repeated again and again ;
Till from outrage—could anything well be absurder ?—
The people all thought I'd committed a murder !
I was hustled about mid the rising cry
Of " scoundrel! brute! into custody !
Away with him! "   Forthwith a stalwart bobby
Produced some handcuffs : " Ha ! now he looks nobby ! "
And such-like phrases were bandied around
As I felt my wrists being rigidly bound.

I was about to be marched straight off to the station
With as noisy a crowd as ever salvation
Lads and lasses drew—when the line along
What should come snorting right into the throng
But that poodle-dog—now here was a puzzle !—
And, yes, I declare ! clapped into his muzzle
Was my dear old briar !—the lady on fire

Had a fit right off—I knew she would,
Or at least I knew she would if she could,
And the crowd's attention being turned to her,
For she made a great fuss, though she couldn't stir,
It gave me the chance at length to explain
What really had happened inside the train.

My story I've told—you can hardly believe
That a dog a man's pipe could so ably retrieve,
And I quite forgave the lady and him
For what had nearly a sequel so grim—
Indeed I offered what I could afford
For that poodle-dog, but I give you my word
The lady was seized with another fit
At hearing the mere suggestion of it,
And so I had to go home contented
With my briar so beautifully coloured and scented.

MR. AND MRS. SMITH

A conventional state of connubial bliss
Is a state that a good many gentlefolk miss;
Some wrangle and fight from morning till night,
Some keep up an outward show of communion,
Though inwardly there is nought but disunion;
But with Mr. and Mrs. Plantaganet Smith—
A fine combination for conjuring with—
The usual tiffs and the usual quarrels
Led only to "makings up" under the laurels;
And so the world thought that they lived as they ought,
Which can't be asserted of every couple
Whose bands are too often a great deal too supple.

But though in this happy and humdrum condition
That betokened a real and close coalition,
Mrs. Smith could not shake herself free from suspicion;

For jealousy's fangs and all the sharp pangs
That spring in due course from that monster's harangues
Ate into her life, and wherever he went
Whatever the purpose on which he was bent
Though he did just nothing at all to arouse
The green-eyed fiend—she followed her spouse
For fear he should stray from the strait-laced way
And the well-kept paths of propriety's sway.

Now it happened one morn, as ill luck would have it,
Mr. Smith had to swear a small affidavit
Before some big beak, who was some way to seek,
When a letter arrived in a feminine hand—
There was no doubt about the caligraphy—and
Mrs. Smith having turned it all corners about
Determined to turn it at length inside out,
Curiosity jealousy's feelings abetting,
Though she felt it was right at the truth to be getting;
So the seal forthwith, though to Mr. Smith
The letter was plainly addressed, she broke,
Half scenting a flame in this small puff of smoke,
And found to her horror, O! Shade of Gomorrah!

That the letter commenced with the words, "My own
  darling,"
And ended, "Yours lovingly, Emily Starling."

Now this was indeed a knock-me-down blow !
To say that her tears rushed forth in a flow
Would but faintly describe the scene that ensued ;
If Miss Starling had come to her straight in the nude
She could'nt have made a greater commotion,
For her *torrents* of tears would have drowned the whole
  ocean,
While her wrath and her rage befitting a demon
Caused a tempest that would have outwitted a seaman.

I should like to explain, to avoid confusion,
And prevent you from forming a wrongful conclusion,
That of all the beneficent beings on earth
To which our creation had ever given birth,
Mr. Smith stood the picture of innocent worth,
So that when he returned and found that his spouse
Was as frantic as one coming fresh from carouse
And her temper just bordering—the reverse of
  soft-sawdering—

On a seething state of eruption volcanic,
While her body displayed a motion galvanic,
The whole of which crashed with terrific explosion,
Like an overcharged barrel that's burst from corrosion,
He was naturally somewhat amazed at its force
For he hadn't the remotest idea of the source,
Though it seemed to the lady a matter of course—
But you must bear in mind, to be just and kind,
When you come to assess his supposed dereliction,
That the weight of the evidence causing the friction
Would have carried to most minds the strongest conviction.

" And so, Mr. Smith," the lady began,
" You've been hatching in secret a dastardly plan
" To deprive of her rights your innocent wife
" Who never did you any harm in her life,
" You who boast in your veins the blood of Plantaganets,
" To take up with your Emilies, Susan Janes, Madge Annettes.
" But you and your hussies may take themselves off,
" I'm not fashioned to be the neighbourhood's scoff ;
" Its all very fine your looking so innocent,
" On your looks I don't set such a store as to pin a cent ;

" You ought to feel shame to dishonour a name
" That's known through the length and breath of the land ;
" I never knew aught so right underhand
" In all my born days—get along with you, Sir !
" You shall never on my good name cast a slur,
" I'll never play second—to none of your hussies."—
But here Mr. Smith begged to ask what this fuss is
About, for his head was all swimming and giddy,
And he felt like a top, or at least like a middy
Who is sent to the top-gallant-mast for the first time,
Which in the Queen's Navy is reckoned the worst time,
And he wasn't quite sure if his lady her senses
Was in, for he knew not of any offences
He'd been guilty of,—no,—it was very mysterious,
For though he well knew she was sometimes imperious,
Which perhaps is not after all deleterious,
'Twas rather her habit to pose as a martyr,
And he'd never yet seen her so like a she-Tartar,
And what could be up he couldn't conjecture—
'Tis sometimes a difficult task to detect your
Fond spouse's intention—so his height of invention

Was to try what he could to quiet his better half,
And if fortune poked fun at him, why just to let her laugh.

But eruptions volcanic are not lightly stilled,
And a lady is often a little self-willed,
And the two things combined made a storm for two
    whole days,
Which, as Mr. Smith said, were just the two sole days
In the length of his married life—now twenty years—
That were shorn of enjoyment; but what between tears,
Which rained off and on like a tropical shower,
And storms, like monsoons, that raged by the hour,
The peace that had reigned for so lengthy a space
Was terribly broken—'twas like a mill race
That dashed over rocks—and so might she storm on,
Believing her husband an ill-disguised Mormon,
For aye and a day, were it not for a chance
Which suddenly put an end to her prance,
For just as the lady's tongue fully nineteen
To the dozen was going, and poor Smith in the mean-
Time, for fear apoplexy should now supervene,
Had brought sal volatile, brandy and salts,
To administer deftly between the tongue's halts,

Which never occurred, the antidote came
In the shape of a note with handwriting the same
As had caused in this peaceful dovecote such a flutter
And occasioned so very unwonted a splutter;
This, in place of "My darling," began "My dear sir,"
And ran on "My note must have made your blood stir,
But the fact is that in a great hurry I put—
I beg you'll forgive what was penned at the foot—
The letter into its wrong envelope—
I trust you'll forgive me and very much hope
It caused no annoyance." Then it was Mr. Smith
Saw the sun through the storm, and the letter forthwith
He read to his spouse, and addressed her, "My dear,
" When you break by mistake a seal, without fear
" Bring it straight to your John ; you see by this letter
" That such a frank course would have been a deal better;
" But mistakes will occur, e'en in conjugal bliss ;
" So say not a word, but just you take this ! "
And he sealed the new bond with a good hearty kiss.

THE CAT

Playmate of childhood, pretty purring puss,
What though you tear the ribbons from her hat
And spoil mamma's best ménu à la Russe,
There's a deal of consolation in a cat!

The boy with well-trained terrier at heel
Searches the shrubs—I wonder what he's at!
"Loo, Tiger, at him!" Then a long-drawn squeal.
There's a deal of satisfaction in a cat!

The sportsman, beating up the cover on the hill,
Spies out the form where Pussy erstwhile sat;
Anon a bang—a scurry—all is still.
Oh! yes! there's satisfaction in a cat!

The married couple locked in slumber deep
Start at a cry—you're not surprised at that—
But baby nestles in the sweetest sleep,
It is, why, yes, it is that beastly cat!

The agitator from the hustings hurling mud
At half the human race, men, women, brats,
At length receives his due with rasping thud.
There's a heap of satisfaction in dead cats!

Old age, forgetting blindly who is who,
Keeps fourteen pussies stretched upon the mat;
You scent a reminiscence of the Zoo?
But yet there's consolation in a cat!

And when the smoking pie is brought to view,
With coney-seeming members rich and fat,
What matters it the least to me or you
If half the dainty bits are pussy-cat?

Then let us give one hearty shout of thanks
In brimming bumpers from the steaming vat;
I care not whether he a Persian be or Manx,
Our loving toast shall be: "Poor Pussy-Cat!"

JOHN CHINAMAN'S PASTRY.

A useful man is our friend, John Chinaman,
Robust and strong, he would make a good miner-man;
Always ready to work, Australia's gardens
He tills on behalf of those Enoch Ardens
Who have left the old country in search of more pelf,
Or, as each would put it, to better himself;
But the John I knew was an excellent cook
Not nurtured on Marshall's cookery-book,
For it doesn't read backwards remarkably well,
And that's the queer way that these Chinamen spell.

Now of all the things our notable *chef*
Excelled in was pastry, which, judging by "Geoff,"
The station manager, was something too light,
For 'twas marvellous how it vanished from sight;
Indeed it was made of such gossamer texture
That, had you a palate, 'twould surely have vexed you.

Innermost soul to watch that old glutton,

Who couldn't distinguish betwixt beef and mutton,

Pass it down in handfuls—light and crisp,

It disappeared like a will of the wisp,

While many and loud were the praises we sounded

Of Chinaman John and the pastry he pounded.

But how did he do it? 'Twas a secret he kept,

And however so deftly behind him we crept

In the kitchen to take a peep at him working,

And although he was never espied his task shirking,

Not a soul had been able to get the least sign

Of how he contrived that pastry divine;

And if asked straight out to show us the way,

His finger would fly to his nose as he'd say,

" Me show you all right—but on some other day ! "

So it ended in nothing, for that other day

Proved always to be such a distance away

That it never advanced appreciably nearer,

Though the pastry meanwhile grew dearer and dearer,

And John in our hearts reached a very warm place,

For we thought him indeed the pick of the race,

Barring Li the astute, the cunning and cute,

Whose jacket was promptly exchanged for the boot

When he reached his own home once more to take root,

Though Li all the same was a jolly good fellow

And looked very well in his jacket of yellow—

But this by the way; Now in our bush station

Where few would have looked for a snug situation,

There happpened to be by way of a treat

A nice little lady's maid, dapper and neat,

Who found the same place in John Chinaman's heart

As he'd gained in our own; and to make him impart

The secret that he professed it to be,

Like Samson's Delilah, she went to John Chinaman,

Though Samson, I trust, was a very much finer man,

All dimpled her face and a smile on her lips,

And, daintily poising her hands on her hips,

Looked up in his face and said, " Mr. John,

Please to put your very best manner on,

And tell me—now do!—how on earth it is you

Can make such fine pastry! You say you're my lover

And to prove it the secret you'll have to discover,

Or never again will I to my John speak; "
And she looked so demure, with her tongue in her che
That John Chinaman melted and said that he would
Most certainly do the best that he could;
If she'd step to the table, she then would be able
To watch every movement of finger and hand
And then without doubt she would quite understand.
So John set to work to mix up the flour
And sprinkled the water in a nice little shower
From a cup that was standing at elbow and handy,
And then he began the mixture to bandy
In the usual way with unusual skill,
And some excellent pastry came out at his will.

But John was crafty, as Chinamen are,
And the maid standing there was really as far
From learning his secret as you are, my friend,
And the séance would there have been at an end,
Had not John's big heart made a thumping start,
And his love and his conscience conniving together
As sun and rain do in true April weather,

He was filled with remorse at that moment, and so
Just as his dear maid was turning to go,
He wickedly winked and was heard to say,
"Me show you, my dear, a more better way."

Now a Chinaman's way, be he ever so bland,
Is a thing that no man can well understand,
Though I'm far from asserting he works underhand ;
But certain it is that under his smiling
There lurks the craftiest art of beguiling,
And " the heathen Chinee " was but an example
Of the product of China that serves as a sample
Of the Eastern methods of artful contrivance
In which the pure Western has little connivance.
So the stranger it is that to this little maid
Our John should have such a great compliment paid
As to throw down his cards and exhibit the trump
That ended alas ! in his getting the " slump."

Having quietly gone and shut to the door
And arranged his utensils the same as before,

He took some fresh flour in the orthodox manner
And blinked his pig eye at his beautiful Hannah,
As into his mouth the contents of the cup
He tipped as he tilted the article up ;
Then holding the water within his lips tight
And mixing the flour with hands supple and light
He was able to squirt the liquid upon it,
Never ceasing to keep his supple hands on it,
With the requisite trickle, neither too slow
Nor too fast—my friend, did ever you know
Such an excellent way of keeping in play
The kneaded flour, for the secret is speed
And rapidity, as I would have you take heed.

The dinner that day was brisk and amusing,
Though the clatter of knives was a trifle confusing,
But as soon as the pastry was placed on the table
The clang of the tongues grew into a babel ;
For the maid disgusted at what she had seen
Had instructed the ladies—perhaps it was mean
Her faithful lover to give thus away,
But the best woman's tongue must needs have its say

And as soon as the pastry appeared, with one screech
The ladies shrieked out and began to beseech
The men to keep it quite out of their reach ;
With the Chinaman present they dare not aver
The cause why their tongues should make such a stir ;
They could only repeat with winks and grimaces
And the pulling of very unladylike faces
As they half arose in dismay from their places,
" Don't, please, it's not nice!" but the men not so squeamish
Disregarded the hints and with faces all beamish
Declared they had never in all their blessed lives,
In despite of the clamour and fuss of their wives,
Enjoyed such a feast—they couldn't make out
What on earth the fair sex could be thinking about
Of such excellent pastry to make such a rout!

John having retired and the dinner being over,
And the men having dined, as they thought, in rare clover,
The ladies were able at length to disclose
The facts, as a scene of confusion arose ;
For some declined to believe the tale,
While others again at the thought turned pale,

As the food that they'd relished some minutes before

Compelled them to make themselves scarce through the
    door;

While others again not to care pretended

And clever John Chinaman's pastry defended—

As long as 'twas good they cared not a fig,

They said, if he'd danced upon it a jig;

It was just as well, if we wished to be wise

Our food not to scan, much less scrutinise,

Which would often no doubt occasion surprise;

The fault, if there was one, lay in our knowing it,

Not at all in the making, but in the man's showing it—

And much further argument of the same sort,

But 'twas noticed that none of the arguers thought

It wise to touch John's pastry again,

Who was very soon moved to a different plane,

Having doubtless taken to heart this moral—

If possessed of a pearl or even a coral

Don't cut it in half, lest its value be lost,

As you will eventually find to your cost;

And if your transaction should ever be shady,

Don't go and impart the fact to a lady;

'Twould be better almost to employ the town-crier,

Or to tell you the truth engage a born liar.

No—to be clever is useless unless you're discreet,

But this is as plain as a giant's two feet,

And such truths it is waste of good time to repeat.

ON COURTSHIPS

I think that man who has never proposed
In a musty museum should be enclosed;
If only for once in his life he ought,
I think, to that critical state to be brought.
Some bring it out with a hearty buss,
Beginning in bliss, though they end with a " cuss ";
Some splutter it out with no end of a fuss,
And some would raise in a vixen a smile,
As gently, but firmly, they're coaxed o'er the stile;
While others again to ink have resort,
Or down on their knees have wrestled and fought;
Indeed, if a goose you wish to see loose,
Just look at the man who flops down on the gravel
In that elegant posture his woes to unravel;
But the man who declines even once to propose
Deserves hanging up by the end of his nose,

Or some other punishment fixed by the fair sex,
Who know what is due to Dame Nature and their sex.

Now a friend of mine had given his heart
The very same day that he purchased a cart,
Which in India's known as a " tum-tum "—the name
Is important, if you will but follow my aim.
Well, the lady of late from Old England had come,
And never had heard of this famous "tum-tum,"
So what was her great surprise and disgust,
At a party of friends, when her lover had just
Proposed for her hand, to hear him say
In a quite unconcerned and natural way,
As he softly bent over, " If with me you will come
Round the corner, my love, you shall see my tum-tum—
I've painted it blue."   The lady arose,
And lifting aloft her dear little nose,
She left her fond lover to stew in his juice,
Disdaining to offer one word of abuse.
On such tiny threads is our life suspended,
That at one little word, by no means intended,

Which could never a delicate ear have offended,
All the pleasures we feel on this planet are ended.

You've heard the name of " Golf " before,
That is sadly played by the sad sea shore ?
Some call it " Gowf," some call it " Goff,"
It depends if you are a " Pro " or a " Toff."
But yet 'tis a game that in modern days,
In all sorts of places and all sorts of ways,
Is played from Caithness to Land's End and from Lancaster
To the best of all Links, which you know are at Brancaster.
It consists in striking a very small ball,
So small you can scarcely see it at all,
Into a small hole that is hardly visible,
Four inches or so is all that's permissible,
With a set of crooked clubs uncouthly constructed
For getting the ball to the hole conducted,
Which makes one emit a word most unfit
To write down in ink without falter or blink,
Beginning with " d " and ending with ——
Which you're certain to say when your club goes smash,

So I make my apology, as it's contra-theology—

Well, Sally was always demure and proper,

In reeling off texts there was no one could top her,

Indeed 'twas a very queer business to stop her,

Which is all very nice in an embryo bride,

As it's likely to cease when the knot has been tied.

But I took my Sally to witness this game,

For I fancied myself a wee bit at the same.

I placed the small ball on its own little tee,

It appeared almost to be smiling at me ;

Then I made a mighty prodigious slam

With a club that was made for the King of Siam,

When off flew its head, and out flew—well, Maam—

'Twas a rush I was quite unable to dam,

And I heard behind me a coughiug—a-hem !

But for all I was worth I couldn't it stem ;

I murmured some phrases about a slip,

But I saw an ominous curl of the lip,

And a turn of the heel, and I gently sighed,

For I knew it meant the turn of the tide,

And that I had lost for ever my bride.

I once had a friend—his name was Stoner—
For his doleful singing we called him " The Moaner "—
Who fell over ears in love with a lass,
And the lass loved him as it came to pass ;
But, although he'd gone in heart and soul for the race,
He couldn't be dragged to the sticking place,
For six-foot high is sometimes as shy
As a schoolgirl who catches her mistress's eye ;
So papa and mamma on either side,
Old Stoner's parents and those of the bride,
Determined that, as they seemed pretty well suited,
The match in due course should be firmly rooted ;
So one day when the pair were shily seated
Unmindful of how they were going to be treated,
The dutiful parents from each side the house
Stole up to the door, and, still as a mouse,
Just turned the key and left them there
Till they were able with truth to declare,
Though perhaps they scarcely enjoyed the fun,
Through the keyhole chink, that the deed was done.